I0810727

THREE COMMUNION HYMNS

for solo piano

Table of Contents

© Copyright 2016 by Fred Bock Music Company. All Rights Reserved. Made in U.S.A.

O SACRED HEAD, NOW WOUNDED

HANS LEO HASSLER
Arranged by FRED BOCK

© Copyright 2016 by Fred Bock Music Company. All rights reserved.

13
mf
16
rit.
a tempo
ten.
mp
p
ten.
19
ten.
mp
ten.
22
mf
25
ten.
mp
mf
ten.

Optional Segue
rit.

COME SHARE THE LORD

BRYAN JEFFERY LEECH
Arranged by FRED BOCK

© Copyright 2016 by Fred Bock Music Company. All rights reserved.

16
a tempo
20
24
28
31

34
37
brighter
mf
(echo)
41
45
49

53
p
ten.
ten. ten. ten.
mf
mf mp p
ten. ten. ten.
a little brighter
mf
57
f
60
mf
slowing
63
ten. ten.
a tempo
mf
no ritard
67
Optional Seque
mf
rit.

WERE YOU THERE?

Spiritual
Arranged by FRED BOCK

© Copyright 2016 by Fred Bock Music Company. All rights reserved.

16
f
dim. poco a poco
20
p
23
mp
26
ten.
mf
Melody
mp
30

34
Melody
f
mf
38
mp
41
p
mp
44
ten.
Jubilantly
f
47
pp
8va
f

50
53
ff
mf
56
59
62
mf
8va
p
l.h.
rit.
r.h.
p